Everything You Need to Know About

Meditation

Meditation can help you improve your health, reduce stress and anxiety, and gain inner happiness and peace of mind.

Everything You Need to Know About
Meditation

Judith Sainte Croix

The Rosen Publishing Group, Inc.
New York

This book is dedicated to Marcelo

Published in 2002 by The Rosen Publishing Group, Inc.
29 East 21st Street, New York, NY 10010

Copyright © 2002 by The Rosen Publishing Group, Inc.

First Edition

All rights reserved. No part of this book may be reproduced in any form without permission in writing from the publisher, except by a reviewer.

Thanks to all of those who generously shared their meditation experiences during this project. Special thanks to Nancy Allison and Sally Freeman for their professional expertise and support, and Joann Jovinelly, who edited this book.

The following meditations appeared in *Meditations for Joy and Creativity* by Judith Sainte Croix © 1997 by Judith Sainte Croix and are reprinted with permission of the publisher, Sonora House Publishing, 484 West 43rd Street, Suite 44-Q, New York, New York 10036: "Creative Visualization for Reaching a Goal," which is an adaptation of "Goal Setting with the Goddess Diana," "Freedom from Fear," "Garden of Happiness," and "Meeting an Inner Guide," which is an adaptation of "Journey to the Isle of the Wise One." Permission is granted by Sonora House Publishing for the home practitioner to record these meditations for their personal use only.

Note to the Reader:
Please do not use any meditations while driving a vehicle or operating equipment. Use these meditation exercises in a safe environment. This book is not to be used as a substitute for proper professional care of any kind. While it is our intention to provide helpful, positive content and the guidance in this book is appropriate in most cases, the author and publisher cannot accept legal responsibility for any problems arising from experimentation with these exercises.

Library of Congress Cataloging-in-Publication Data

Croix, Judith Sainte.
Everything you need to know about meditation / Judith Sainte Croix.
p. cm. — (The need to know library)
Includes bibliographical references and index.
ISBN 978-1-4358-8844-9
1. Meditation. I. Title. II. Series.
BL627 .C76 2001
158.1'2—dc21

2001002701

Manufactured in the United States of America

Contents

	Introduction	6
Chapter 1	Beginning the Art of Meditation	9
Chapter 2	Mantras, Chanting, Chakras, and Creative Visualization	17
Chapter 3	The Ancient Origins of Meditation	25
Chapter 4	Supportive Meditation	35
Chapter 5	A Day of Joy and Wisdom	48
	Glossary	56
	For More Information	60
	For Further Reading	62
	Index	63

Introduction

You may have seen pictures of famous people, such as the Beatles, sitting cross-legged with gurus, or spiritual guides, in Far Eastern countries or heard about Gandhi using meditation in his nonviolent plan to liberate India from England. Perhaps while watching television you have seen the Dalai Lama from Tibet, in his saffron and yellow robes, and you have heard that he practices the art of meditation.

You may be wondering what meditation is. Maybe you are a seeker, someone who looks for ways to make your life happier and more balanced. Or you may be a very active person who wonders why anyone would want to practice meditation because it appears to be a waste of time. Maybe you have already tried meditation techniques and you want additional information.

The Dalai Lama chants in a praying position during a teaching session at UCLA in Los Angeles, California.

Meditation is a broad subject and covers a wide range of activities, from exercises in which you sit very still, to methods based on movement, to meditations used for sports and other activities. People try meditation for many reasons. Some of these reasons may include gaining inner happiness and peace of mind, improving a sense of health and spirituality, reducing the body's level of stress and anxiety, or becoming a more disciplined and focused individual.

Meditation is a tool that an individual can use to help control his or her body, mind, and spirit. It can bring insight, peace, and energy to any man, woman, or child. Everyone has access to the power of meditation.

Meditation

Meditation can be different for everyone, and it is usually a very individualized experience. For many, meditation allows a person to bypass the daily chatter of the mind to connect with his or her inner self. And as you will read in this book, the methods and styles of meditation are as different and varied as the many different cultures of people on this planet.

In answering the question, "What is meditation?" Joseph Goldstein and Jack Kornfield tell this ancient story from the Buddhist tradition in their book *Seeking the Heart of Wisdom*. Soon after his enlightenment, as the Buddha was walking down a road, he passed a man who noticed his peace and radiance. The man asked him if he was a god, a magician, or a wizard.

The Buddha replied, "No."

"Well then, what are you?" asked the man.

"I am awake," said the Buddha.

Meditation is listening to the Divine within.
—Edgar Cayce

Chapter 1: Beginning the Art of Meditation

There are common misconceptions about meditation that can keep people from trying it. Some people think you have to go to a monastery or to another religious place to meditate. The truth is that anyone can meditate anywhere, and at anytime. Other people are concerned that meditating might conflict with their religious beliefs. But meditation is a state of mind, not a religion. While meditation is often a practice of a particular religion, it is not necessary to join that religion or change your religious beliefs in order to meditate.

The simple act of meditation is an internal act of cultivating the mind and is often called "mindfulness." In the words of the Buddha, "Meditation untangles what is tangled." Many people equate the idea of meditation

Meditation

with a concentrated level of spiritual consciousness. To meditate is to rid the mind of distracting thoughts. In this way the individual can detach from thought, thus allowing the sense of inner peace and oneness that is deep within ourselves to surface. To meditate is to learn how to experience something deeper than thought. Only then is it possible to experience a feeling of inner peace and oneness with yourself and the world around you. Some people believe that practicing meditation helps heal the soul, sharpen the mind, and rejuvenate the spirit. For many others, meditation, because of its ability to easily calm the mind, serves as a simple practice to provide relief from stress and anxiety.

Some people prefer to join a meditation group, where they learn to do meditative exercises that guide them in developing qualities of wisdom, creativity, and focused attention. Still others use chanting and breathing as a form of meditation to relieve stress. Meditation can develop and maintain a state of mind that is free, relaxed, open, and alert.

Calming the Mind

The paths to meditation are varied, but they have at least one common goal: calming the mind. Whether you are a Tibetan monk, an African tribal holy man, an athlete using visualization to improve a high jump, or a beginning yoga student, the first goal of meditation is

Athletes often use meditation and visualization techniques to improve their performances.

Meditation

to calm, or still, the mind. Calming the mind can be achieved simply by sitting still, closing the eyes, and breathing slowly and deeply.

In meditation, you are taught to calm the mind and focus it solely on an object. If your mind strays away from the object of meditation toward other distracting thoughts, you should gently lead it back to its point of origin. In the stilling the mind meditation, you will use your breath as the object of the meditation.

Meditation Exercise No. 1: Stilling the Mind

1. Sit in a comfortable position, in a chair or cross-legged on the floor. Let your hands rest on your legs.

2. Close your eyes and focus your mind on breathing.

3. Breathe slowly, in and out from your abdomen.

4. Count ten slow breaths in and out. If thoughts come into your mind as you count the breaths, don't try to stop them or focus on them. Let any thoughts or ideas float through your mind like clouds.

Beginning the Art of Meditation

> 5. When you finish the ten breaths, sit in silence for a minute.

Developing a Meditation Practice

If you have just done this meditation exercise, you have taken the first step to developing a daily meditation practice. When developing this practice, it is best to meditate every day. You can increase the time that you meditate each day until you meet your goal. Some people meditate for ten to twenty minutes, twice per day. During days when you cannot do your full practice, you can still meditate for one or two minutes. By keeping this schedule your body and mind will remain sharp, and the benefits of meditation will be available to you whenever you need them.

Generally, it is a good idea to find a quiet place in which to meditate. Find a convenient place, inside or outside, that you can devote to your daily practice. Arrange objects around your special area that enhance your meditative state of mind, such as fragrant candles or incense, pictures of mentors or spiritual guides, or objects such as flowers, rocks, shells, or crystals that are inspirational to you. Meditating outdoors in a natural setting, such as near a lake can also be inspiring if the spot is private and secluded.

It is not necessary to sit in the lotus position in order to meditate.

Beginning the Art of Meditation

Monitoring the passage of time during your daily meditation practice is useful so that you can meditate more freely. Another time-keeping technique is to record the instructions for your favorite meditation on a cassette tape or to use a timer. Many people choose a specific time of day to meditate, such as in the morning or just before bed. Others have a very irregular approach and may never develop a meditation pattern. Generally speaking, meditation may be done during any time of the day or night.

When many people think of the art of meditation, they imagine someone sitting in the lotus position, in which the feet are brought to rest on the thighs in a cross-legged fashion. But while sitting in the full or half lotus position or simply sitting cross-legged with the hands resting on the knees is generally the style in yoga and Zen meditations, it is not necessary to remain in any position that is uncomfortable in order to meditate. Cushions and stools can also be used to make sitting cross-legged more comfortable, or meditation can be done sitting in a chair. Occasionally, meditations are even done lying down.

Finally, you can meditate alone or in a group during a meditation class. Some people find that they like the feeling of the group's energy. Others prefer the solace that solitary meditation provides.

Controlling Your Thoughts

Sometimes people experience negative or limiting thoughts without even being aware of them. These thoughts are playing over and over in the background of our minds, like faintly audible music. Some people ignore these thoughts, while others are the helpless victims of them. Good or bad, we are not always in control of our mind's reflections. However, the act of meditation may help you control unwanted thought patterns.

The mind generates positive and negative thoughts all the time. Meditation helps us choose the thoughts that are best for us. In order to take charge of our constant thought patterns, we need to become more aware. Then we can choose what to focus on, rather that allowing our minds to wander aimlessly. A meditation practice increases our awareness of our thoughts at all times.

We are what we think. All that we are arises with our thoughts.
—The Buddha

Chapter 2

Mantras, Chanting, Chakras, and Creative Visualization

When we can focus on words and sounds as the object of a meditation, it is called a mantra. Sometimes the words are chanted purely for their sound rather than their actual meaning. The vibrations of the sound create a resonance in the body. Mantras are based on this physical vibration. For some people, mantras are prayers or sacred thoughts.

The actual word "mantra" is derived from a phrase in the ancient Indian language of Sanskrit and means "a tool of thought," according to Lorin Roche, Ph.D., in his book *Meditation Made Easy*.

Sogyal Rinpoche, in his book *The Tibetan Book of Living and Dying*, says, "Each syllable [of the mantra] is impregnated with spiritual power. Each condenses a spiritual truth and vibrates with a blessing. When you chant a mantra, you are charging your breath and energy with the energy of that mantra."

Meditation

Meditation Exercise No. 2: Mantra Chanting

Om Mani Padme Hum (pronounced "ohm mah nee pahd may hum") is both a Hindu and a Buddhist mantra of compassion. Chanting it enhances your positive feelings toward all things.

1. Sit in a comfortable position. Close your eyes. Center and focus your attention by breathing slowly. Inhale and exhale from your nostrils several times.

2. Begin repeating the mantra, Om Mani Padme Hum. Use the lowest register of your voice. Continue repeating this mantra for five minutes.

3. Sit in silence. Notice the calming effects of the chanting.

Meditation Exercise No. 3: Chanting Hu

Chanting Hu (pronounced like the word "hue") is a spiritual exercise practiced in Eckankar, the Religion of the Light and Sound of God.

Mantras, Chanting, Chakras, and Creative Visualization

1. Sit in a comfortable position. Closing your eyes, concentrate on the "third eye," a point roughly above, and between, your eyebrows. (The third eye supports a person's desire to connect with thoughts that are beyond him or her.)
2. Sing "Hu" in one long breath. Repeat slowly for ten to twenty minutes.

Chakras

The third eye mentioned in the last exercise is one of the seven chakras, or centers, within the body. This system, originating in the practice of yoga, views the body as a constellation of energy fields imagined as wheels of light. Some people imagine these energy fields as spinning wheels or vortexes. In meditation practices, the positive development and interaction between the chakras helps revitalize physical, mental, and emotional health.

There is a growing sense within the alternative healing community that acupuncture, acupressure, and shiatsu, which use meridians to chart the body's energy paths, have a relationship to the energetic healers' understanding of the chakras and invisible bodies.

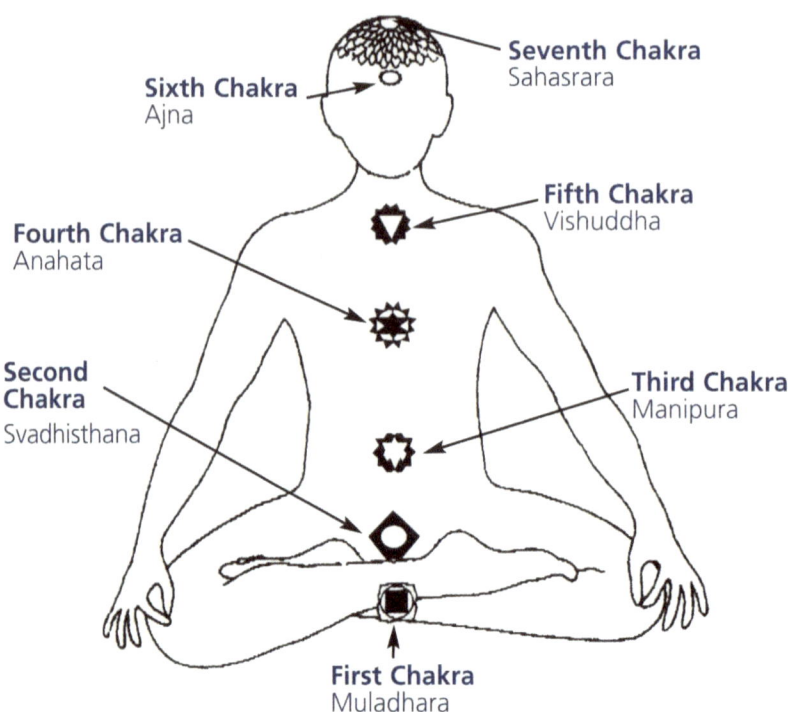

The lowest chakra, located at the root of the spine, symbolizes the body's energy; the second is symbolic for balance, and is located at the sacral plexus near the reproductive organs; and the third, associated with self-esteem, is at the solar plexus near the navel. The fourth chakra is located at the heart and is said to govern compassion; the fifth is located at the throat and is symbolic of self-expression; and the sixth at the third eye (located between and just above the eyebrows) represents wisdom. The last chakra, the seventh, is located at the top of the head and represents the body's center of spirituality. The Sanskrit names and color associations of the chakras are, respectively, muladhara (red), svadhishthana (orange), manipura (yellow), anahata (green), vishuddha (sky blue), ajna (indigo), and sahasrara (white).

Some think that by drawing hunting scenes on cave walls, ancient hunters increased their chances of having successful hunts.

Creative Visualization

Creative visualization is a form of meditation in which one imagines scenes and pictures in the mind during meditation. Words that create images and evoke memories in the mind guide the person on an inner journey. It is a very ancient form of meditation. Some people believe that drawings inside prehistoric caves are examples of creative visualization. Perhaps by drawing scenes of a successful hunt on the cave wall, hunters increased their chances of bringing home a hearty dinner.

Meditation

This is also known as manifestation, an act in which people create pictures in their imagination of things they want to create. By meditating on those pictures, they enhance their ability to "manifest" things—to make the desired results appear in the material world.

In the next exercise, you are going to do creative visualization. You will go on an inner journey to visit the mythological hunter, the goddess Diana in an ancient, primeval forest. She is often called by different names in different cultures. Diana is her Roman name. Her ability to hit the target in the hunt symbolizes that part of us that sets and reaches clearly articulated goals.

Meditation Exercise No. 4: Creative Visualization for Reaching a Goal

1. **A part of the creative visualization process is preparing your space for the most rewarding, imaginative experience. For this particular visualization, bathe and fill the room with scents of lavender, bergamot, and patchouli incense on the night of the full moon.**

Mantras, Chanting, Chakras, and Creative Visualization

Light three white candles that will burn as a symbol of both clarity and purity. In this exercise, you will be concentrating on one particular goal that you would like to complete.

2. On a piece of paper, write the goal for which you seek inspiration and wisdom from the goddess Diana, such as gaining employment, writing a song, or running a marathon. Sit in front of your candles and breathe in and out three times from the heart center, the fourth chakra. This chakra supports your intuition. Pause. Imagine a circle of white light surrounding and protecting you. Pause. Next, imagine a cord of golden light that extends from the base of your spine to the center of the earth. This cord firmly grounds you to the planet's core.

3. In your imagination, move along a path that leads from your home to the primeval forest. Pause.

Meditation

4. Using your imagination, visualize the goddess Diana in full detail. She listens as you speak of your goals. Pause. She gives practical advice. Pause. Together, you create a plan to realize your goals. Pause. Her important qualities include strength, honesty, kindness, intelligence, skill, compassion, and others. Pause.

5. Although eternally young, the goddess Diana is ancient and knowledgeable. Visualize yourself succeeding in that goal. Pause.

6. When your visualization exercise is completed, remain in silence for a moment. Sit calmly in the candlelight.

Chapter 3
The Ancient Origins of Meditation

Now that you have tried some meditations, you may want to know something about the ancient origins of this practice. After a lifetime of studying world myth and religion, the scholar Joseph Campbell concluded that all people seek to understand the mysteries of life. This idea was recently expressed at an international conference on the subject in 1999, at the invitation of the Karma Ling Buddhist Dharma Center in the French Alps. Traditional spiritual leaders from all over the world gathered to share their beliefs and practices. When shamans from Africa, Siberia, Asia, Mexico, and North and South America, Aborigines from Australia, and practitioners of vodoun (voodoo) from the Caribbean came together to share insights, they agreed on several common points—in particular, the interconnectedness of all things. Meditative practices are often used in this search.

Meditation

Meditation Practices in the East

Eastern philosophies share this belief in spiritual oneness. An idea central to Hinduism, the major religion of India, is that the entire physical and spiritual worlds are united and that all things are interconnected. This is what the Hindus refer to as "the Spiritual Universe."

Yoga, a meditation path associated with Hinduism, is an approach with specific techniques for achieving the peace of mind inherent in the experience of oneness. Today, the practice of yoga is widespread in the Western world. Many health clubs offer classes in hatha yoga, which focuses the mind through a system of physical postures called asanas. These postures have beneficial effects on the internal organs and energy pathways in the body, which are called meridians.

Another Eastern religion that speaks of the interconnectedness of all things is Buddhism. Its central figure, the Buddha, was born a prince named Siddhartha in a kingdom in the foothills of the Himalayas in 563 BC. When he was twenty-nine, he became very concerned with the suffering of the people in his country and set out to find a solution. He tried all of the spiritual paths that were available in an effort to discover why people suffer. Still, he did not find the answers he was seeking.

Tibetan Buddhist priests, seen here, often use visualization, in which one imagines scenes and images in the mind during meditation.

Finally, after meditating for forty-nine days, he received answers to all his questions. According to the story, he experienced complete enlightenment and then took the name Buddha, which is translated as "awakened one." Later, he taught others how to reach enlightenment through meditation and other teaching methods. He discouraged followers, preferring that each person experience his or her own truth. His methods of teaching became known as Buddhism and are still practiced by many people in Asian countries and elsewhere.

The goal of many Buddhists is to strive to be in the world but not of it, meaning that they maintain complete awareness of their thoughts, emotions, and attitudes while interacting in the material world. If they can do this well and maintain a peaceful mind, then they have attained Nirvana, which is not a place, like heaven in the Christian belief system, but a state of mind. Nirvana is a state of complete peace. Meditation is one of the tools Buddhists use in their search for Nirvana. Their goal is to achieve a state of mind in which they are completely aware as they go about their daily activities.

Zen Buddhism began in India and spread to China and then Japan. Roshi Philip Kapleau, in his book *The Three Pillars of Zen*, defines it as "a religious practice with a unique method of body-mind training whose aim is awakening, that is, self-realization."

Buddhism also spread to Tibet. Tibetan Buddhism often uses visualization, a form of meditation in which one imagines scenes and images in the mind during meditation. In one Tibetan-Buddhist meditation, for instance, destructive thoughts of hatred, anger, and jealousy are replaced with thoughts of love and compassion. Meditation exercise number nine on page 46 is a Buddhist-inspired meditation.

China developed forms of meditative exercises, such as tai chi, believed to bring mental, physical, and spiritual benefits to those who practice it. Likewise, the martial arts of the East, based on various fighting skills and movements, also have a meditative component.

The Ancient Origins of Meditation

Meditation Practices in the West

In the 1970s, there was an explosion of interest in meditation in the West. An Indian guru named Maharishi Yogi developed a meditation practice called transcendental meditation that was attractive to Westerners. Even earlier, Swiss psychiatrist Carl Jung (1875–1961) had begun using visualization with his clients. Since then, many people have taken up meditation in the West. This is sometimes referred to as New Age meditation, although many of the techniques being taught are very old.

Eckankar, which means "the way of spirit," is another ancient path of spiritual development that is very active today. Eckankar provides teachings about spiritual exercises developed by a long line of spiritual masters.

Spiritual exercises are a form of contemplation in which the person actively focuses on a spiritual principle, or uses visualization to explore many realities. For an example of a spiritual exercise from Eckankar, see meditation exercise number three on pages 18–19.

In old Europe, as we have learned from the research of archaeologist Marija Gimbutas, the ancient spiritual paths in Europe from around 5000 BC and earlier were defined by societies of

Meditation

agricultural people who communed with gods in order to ensure plentiful crops. Prehistoric people based their religious experiences on natural cycles. In her book, *The Civilization of the Goddess*, Gimbutas says, "the Great Mother Goddess who gives birth to all creation became a metaphor for Nature herself." She discovered a profusion of ceramics, figurines, wall paintings, and ritual articles, symbolizing the Great Goddess. Most of these artifacts dated back to 6500–3500 BC. She discovered that these societies ensured plentiful crops and a good life through meditative rituals. Christianity, when it first spread into these areas, came to the cities. The country people were slow to give up their accustomed worship of nature deities. They became known as *pagani*, which meant country dwellers, or rural folks. From the word "pagani," the term "pagan" was derived, a widespread term for people not converted to Christianity.

Some of these traditions still survive today in a religion called Wicca, which uses chant, mantra, and visualization in its rituals. The rituals are done to bring insights to the devoted that go beyond what can be expressed in words alone. Practitioners of Wicca evoke deities and thereby feel a sense of oneness with all living things, which promotes an understanding of the sacredness of nature.

Wiccans seek a sense of oneness with all living things and promote an understanding of the sacredness of nature.

The religion of Wicca, traditional tribal practices in Africa, shamanism, and some of the branches of major religions all share the belief that the whole cosmos is alive. It is then possible, within this belief system, to become one with the stars, wind, trees, and rocks while in a peaceful, meditative state of mind.

Now that you have an understanding of the ancient origins of meditation, you realize that the practice of mindful, meditative prayer was quite common. One pagan text, *Allogenes*, states that, "There was a stillness of silence within me and I heard the blessedness whereby I knew myself as I am."

Ancient Meditation Practices and Gnosticism

Meditative exercises were also used by the ancient Druids, Greeks, Jewish mystics, the predecessors of Islam in Iran, the worshippers of Ishtar in Babylon, and the Gnostics. Gnosticism, which gets its name from the Greek word for wisdom, *gnosis*, was a meditative spiritual movement just before the time of Christ. Gnosticism fused the mystic approach of the Orient with the rationalism of Greek thought as found in the teachings of Plato and Homer. It taught direct experience of divine inspiration through meditation.

In the mystical branch of Judaism that teaches the Kabbalah, the seeker hopes to transcend the mundane and peek at the divine. To do this, seekers are inspired through guided meditation techniques. Some of these techniques parallel methods found in Zen Buddhism.

All Judaism, Christianity, and Islamic meditation takes the form of prayer. In Sufism, a mystical branch of Islam, prayers take the form of dance. Sufis whirl for long periods of time while repeating sacred phrases and the name of the deity to achieve oneness with the divine.

In Christianity, in the fourth century AD, there was a group of monks known as the desert fathers because of their remote location in the Egyptian desert. They practiced constant repetition of prayer, similar to the practice of chanting mantras in the Eastern religions. By praying constantly, they hoped to attain a purity of heart known as *quies*.

Meditation in North and South America

The meditation techniques used by the indigenous people of North and South America stretch back for centuries. Although the specific meditative practices vary from tribe to tribe, traditional North American Native Americans see spirits in all living things and see themselves as a part of nature. The trees, rocks, animals, wind, rain, clouds, and human beings all have an inner spirit. It is possible to speak to all of them through the act of ceremony, which includes the state of mind defined as meditative. In their worldview, all natural phenomena are part of a spiritual continuum, which must be in balance in order to survive. Traditionally, many North American Native Americans use their dances as a moving meditation, in which prayers are sent via the feet to honor the earth and create universal harmony.

The specific meditative practices also vary from tribe to tribe in South America. One example is the Q'ero tribe of the Andean highlands. They have no concept of "good" and "evil" energy within their belief system. There is only refined "light" energy

Meditation

and its opposition, "heavy" energy. They gain knowledge of how to heal people of their heavy energy through communication with mountain spirits while in meditative states.

The search to understand existence, to participate in deeper layers of reality, and to experience the comfort and bliss of spiritual oneness is a universal human trait that is as old and as widespread as humanity. In the book *Black Elk: The Sacred Ways of a Lakota*, Wallace H. Black Elk explains that in his way of knowing Grandfather (the Sky) is Wisdom and Grandmother (the Earth) is Knowledge, but they are really One. He explains, "Our Father is Tunkashila [the Creator] and our Mother is the Earth. They give birth and life to all the living, so we know we're all interrelated."

Chapter 4

Supportive Meditation

In chapter 3, we explored only a few of the many kinds of meditation practices that exist in the world. Now let's examine how meditation can be used to deal with specific situations or problems.

Affirmations

An affirmation is a positive phrase that you can create as an aid in overcoming difficulty or to enhance your life. An affirmation on any subject is always stated in a positive way. For instance, an affirmation statement could be "I get good grades in math class" rather than "I won't fail in math class." State affirmations in the present tense, such as "My courage is increasing" rather than "I will try to be less fearful."

Affirmations can help your mind focus on more positive things other than depression.

A good time to create powerful affirmations for yourself is when you are not feeling your best. When something is upsetting you, try to discover the thoughts behind the emotions you are feeling. Then you have the raw material necessary to create a truthful and useful affirmation.

For example, if you feel anxious while waiting to hear about a college application, you may be thinking, "I'll never get into college." Create an affirmation that says the opposite. "I am accepted into the school that is right for me."

Or, if you have applied for a job and are fearful of not getting it, say, "I will have the perfect job for me."

Supportive Meditation

If you are always tongue-tied and embarrassed in social situations you can create several affirmations such as, "People enjoy speaking with me." "I am a good listener." "People value my company."

Affirmations activate the subconscious mind to create better thought patterns. By repeating positive, affirmative statements of the results we seek to create, a wealth of favorable information is reinforced in our minds.

The following are several basic affirmations:

- **I deserve love, happiness, and success.**
- **I respect and love my body.**
- **I am a beautiful creation of the universe and I am loved and valued for just being myself.**

Never create phrases that seek to harm others. Always create affirmations about yourself and about ideas and thought patterns that you want to change, rather than about other people you may want to change.

Affirmations help us think positively, build our confidence, and help us to develop faith in ourselves and our lives. Whenever you are facing a challenge, ask yourself: How can I do this? Where can I get help? What is the outcome I want to create? Then, create some affirmations that state your goals as if they have already happened.

Meditation

First, create the affirmation you want to use, such as "I am a successful student." Use that phrase while meditating morning and night for twenty-one days. The repetition of working with an affirmation impresses the positive way of thinking on the mind's subconscious. It is in that way that you will begin to see positive changes.

Meditation Exercise No. 5: Affirmation Meditation

1. Sit in a comfortable position. Close your eyes and focus your mind, creating a feeling of calmness. Breathe slowly and deeply three times.

2. Now repeat your affirmation, either silently or aloud, twenty-one times. Allow yourself to believe that the affirmation is already true. Say it with energy and enthusiasm. If your mind presents you with any reason why this cannot be true, gently lead it back to your original affirmation statement.

3. Finish your meditation with three slow, deep breaths. Open your eyes and sit silently for a moment.

Supportive Meditation

During the day, if doubts and insecurities arise, such as negative thought patterns, substitute your affirmative thoughts for the negative ideas. If you need to, refer to your affirmation by writing it down and carrying it with you. Be alert to all the ways in which your new affirmation is affecting your life.

> *The spirits told me if a bad thought or bad word ever comes to you, to let it go in your ear and out the other ear, but never out your mouth. If it comes out of your mouth it is going to hurt somebody and then that hurt will come back to you twice.*
> —Wallace H. Black Elk
> *Black Elk: The Sacred Ways of a Lakota*

Specific Meditations

For many people, the act of meditation is useful for minimizing stress and anxiety, reducing pain, and achieving a calmer state of mind. Other people use daily meditation exercises to deal with specific problems or troubling times in their lives that require a greater sense of concentration. The following meditations are meant to serve as specific instructions for you to follow. They will help you to develop increased mental focus, which can clear your mind of any uncertain thoughts.

Meditation

Meditation Exercise No. 6: Creative Visualization for Success in Athletics

Like most achievements, competing in sporting events and activities takes control, grace, stamina, endurance, and concentration. Meditation is one way to help you achieve top form as an athletic competitor.

1. Sit or lie in a comfortable position. Imagine each section of your body relaxing. Ease any tension by visualizing a white light that begins in your toes and travels through your body to the top of your head. As it leaves the top of your head, it carries away all tension. Pause.

2. Next, focus your awareness with three deep breaths. Pause.

3. Now put yourself in the setting of the sports activity. Vividly imagine the place, colors, lights, teammates, and spectators. Pause.

4. With an imaginary camera, zoom in on yourself. See yourself performing as a top athlete in peak form. If you have a sports goal that you want to

Supportive Meditation

reach, such as jumping a certain distance or running a mile within a set amount of time, imagine yourself achieving that goal. Visualize yourself performing every detail. For instance, if it's a team sport, imagine hitting a home run, scoring the deciding goal, or catching the fly ball that wins the game. Pause.

5. Now use your camera to focus inside yourself. This camera can peer inside to your feelings and sensations. It prints out a message, like a ticker tape, that tells you all the feelings and sensations that are associated with reaching this goal that you have set for yourself. Focus deeply on those feelings. Pause.

6. In one graceful movement, stretch your arms out and bring all your feelings back inside yourself. Return to your normal state of consciousness. Open your eyes. Sit for a moment and relax in your affirmative state, understanding that you are on your way to greater success.

Meditation

Meditation Exercise No. 7: Creative Visualization for Freedom from Fear

We all experience fear. Fear is useful when it warns us of danger, but very often, fear stops us from doing things we would like to do. When fear stands in your way, try the following meditation.

1. Sit in a comfortable, quiet place. Close your eyes. Focus and calm your mind, taking three deep breaths. Pause. Imagine a white light surrounding you and a cord of golden light that extends from the base of your spine to the center of the earth. Visualize this light as a strong force that helps to ground you during the meditation. Pause.

2. Now focus your attention on the inner sensations of your body. Imagine that you are searching your entire body, noting where the feelings of fear are located in your body. Pause.

3. Next, visualize just one of the places in your body where you sense fear exists. Ask yourself:

Supportive Meditation

If this fear were an object, what would it be? Notice its shape, texture, and form. Describe it. For instance, your fear might appear like a hard, gray rock in your chest, or a piece of plastic stretched between your heart and your stomach. Pause.

4. Visualize an imaginary inner hand that will reach inside your body and pull this fear out and set it in front of you. Pause.

5. It's time to examine your fear. Ask yourself: What is this fear about? What is it related to? Do this as often as necessary until all your fears are exposed to you. Pause.

6. Now imagine a beautiful, sparkling river of light flowing past you. Pause. Toss your fears in that river and let them float away. Imagine that the river is so strong that the fear is destroyed. Pause.

7. Next, remember a time when you acted courageously and overcame your fears. Vividly remember the

Meditation

experience and let the feeling spread like a great star of courage. Pause. Finally, create an affirmation that describes your courage. Pause.

8. Finish the exercise with a chant or prayer of your choice, or by repeating your original affirmation.

Meditation Exercise No. 8: Breathing to Reduce Stress

The following breathing exercise is very calming and greatly reduces anxiety and stress. If you find it difficult to breathe out for eight counts, begin by breathing out for only three counts, and gradually increase the length of your exhale each time.

Begin this stress-reducing meditation practice by lying on a bed or a mat on the floor. Rest your hands on your abdomen.

1. Close your eyes and focus inward.

2. Take slow, relaxing breaths through your nostrils for the count of three seconds. Breathe deeply, filling your abdomen with air. Exhale gently out through the mouth for eight seconds.

Breathing exercises can be a great way to reduce stress and anxiety.

3. Focus on the counting of each set of breaths. If your mind wanders, attempt to bring it back into focus. Concentrate only on controlled breathing.

4. Repeat this breathing exercise fifteen times.

5. Remain relaxed and silent for as long as possible. Open your eyes. Return to your activities with a renewed and calm energy.

Meditation

In the next meditation, you have the opportunity to send positive energy to people that are angry, bothersome, or downright loathsome. Why is it helpful to send positive thoughts to your enemies? Simply because it will give you peace of mind from angry thoughts. Sometimes, it even transforms your relationship with that person.

Meditation Exercise No. 9: Dealing with Difficult People

Sit in a comfortable position. Close your eyes and relax your body.

1. Breathe deeply three times. Repeat these three phrases three times. I am happy. I am healthy. I am safe.

2. Now picture someone you look up to: a mentor, friend, or teacher. Say the same three phrases three more times for that person.

3. Next, picture a neutral person, someone you do not know. For instance, imagine someone you saw on the street and say the same three phrases for them three times.

Supportive Meditation

4. Now turn your attention to the difficult person in your life. As sincerely as you can, say the phrases three times for this person.

5. Finish by repeating the three phrases again for yourself.

6. Sit quietly for a few moments. Notice how you feel. Finish your meditation with three slow, deep breaths. Open your eyes. Relax.

Chapter 5 | A Day of Joy and Wisdom

People who meditate sometimes go on retreats so they can concentrate on meditating without the distractions of daily life, such as working, cooking, or shopping. While at the retreat, they spend the whole day performing different kinds of meditation, such as sitting meditation, walking meditation, creative visualization, chanting, and breathing exercises. They aspire to remain in a state of mindfulness all day and all night. You and your friends can try your own mini-retreat by doing the following practices on a day devoted entirely to meditation.

The great outdoors can serve as a retreat where you can meditate without interruption.

Meditation Exercise No. 10: Creative Visualization in the Garden of Happiness

1. Start your day of meditation with a creative visualization to evoke a state of happiness. Sit comfortably. Close your eyes. Relax your body. Breathe deeply three times. Visualize a golden cord going from the base of your spine into the center of the earth.

Meditation

As in the prior meditations, this cord is grounding you and connecting you to the energy of the earth's core. Pause.

2. Imagine a serene garden. Pause. The entrance to the garden is cluttered with debris. Imagine that the clutter represents all your negative, hopeless, and discouraged thoughts. You notice a tiny, silver vacuum cleaner by your side. You point the nozzle at the debris and suck it up into the vacuum. You empty the debris onto the ground, where it becomes transformed. Pause.

3. Next, imagine walking into the garden and sitting on the bench by a fountain. This is the fountain of happiness. As you look into the water, you experience thoughts, images, and memories of happiness. Let these images of happiness fill your mind. Pause.

4. Feel the deep, inner glow of these images of happiness. Imagine the

A Day of Joy and Wisdom

happiness as a warm light in your heart. This light grows until it fills your entire body and the imaginary garden. Pause.

5. Sit in silence for a moment. When you are ready, slowly open your eyes. You can remember this happiness in your heart at any time during the day.

Meditation Exercise No. 11: Walking Meditation

In many meditation practices, people are encouraged to be active, as in this exercise, where the objective of the meditation is the movement of walking. You should try to find a serene outdoor setting for this exercise.

1. Stand still and become aware of your entire body. As thoughts arise, tell yourself that you will gently return your focus to your body's own movement.

2. Begin moving slowly. Focus on the action of picking up you feet and putting them down.

Meditation

3. Walk five or ten minutes along a path, and then turn and return to where you started.

4. Stand motionless for a moment and notice how you feel. Try to keep that feeling with you for the rest of the day.

Meditation Exercise No. 12: Meditation in Action

In the walking meditation, the focus of the exercise is the movement of the arms and legs while walking. In meditation in action, the focus is whatever movement you are doing.

You can apply this awareness to eating if you want to lose weight, to sports if you want to excel in competition, or to practice if you want to master a musical instrument. An intriguing application is using meditation in action to calm the mind while doing chores, such as cleaning dishes, taking out the garbage, or raking leaves.

Again, Buddhists refer to this idea as mindfulness. You can apply mindfulness by being totally aware and calmly focused on whatever you are doing, whenever you are doing it during your day.

A Day of Joy and Wisdom

Meditation Exercise No. 13: Creative Visualization for Meeting an Inner Guide for Wisdom

Close your day by visiting your own inner guide to wisdom. Each of us has access to our own inner guides. Try this creative visualization to discover yours.

1. Lie down in a comfortable place, close your eyes, and relax your body. Call to mind a problem or situation for which you wish to seek advice.

2. Now use your imagination to travel to the shore of a beautiful blue lake. On the shore, create an imaginary circle with small stones and sit inside. Visualize a golden cord going from the base of your spine into the center of the earth. Pause. Breathe deeply three times. Leave any negative feelings or thoughts in this circle. Send them into the earth to be transformed. Pause. Now, in your imagination, rise and step out of the circle.

Meditation

3. There is a yellow boat on the lake's shore. You get in the boat and travel across the blue water. Pause. After gliding for some time, you arrive at an island. This island is your private place for meeting your inner guide. Imagine climbing a steep bluff and arriving on a high, green, grassy plateau.

4. When you reach the top, look into the distance. Someone is walking toward you. As the person approaches, notice whether they are male or female, his or her appearance, and his or her dress. Pause. Ask his or her name. Pause. Sit with this person in the grass. Ask him or her for advice. Pause.

5. Climb back down the bluff, get in the boat, and reflect upon your experiences on the island as you travel back to the other shore. Pause.

6. When you get to the other shore, you see your circle of stones. Pick the stones up, and put them in

A Day of Joy and Wisdom

your pocket. You notice flowers are now growing where you left your negative thoughts and feelings. The journey is complete. Know that you can return to your private island to speak with your inner guide at any time. Pause.

7. Return your focus to your body. Feeling the surface beneath you, stretch and gradually open your eyes. When you are ready, slowly rise and sit silently for a few moments.

Finding Your Path

As you explore and try paths of meditation, you will find the one that is right for you. Meditation can help you see that you are not only your body, mind, or emotions. Beyond this, you are a wonderful, creative being. You have been given the precious gift of life with which to experience and explore the universe. Meditation is a tool that can guide you, helping you to bring the gift of your unique self into the world.

Glossary

affirmation Positive phrase.

asana Term that means steady pose; posture used in the practice of yoga.

Buddha Founder of Buddhism.

chakras Energy centers in the body seen as wheels of light. They are the points where the physical and spiritual aspects of the body meet.

Christianity Major religion based on the teachings of Jesus Christ.

compassion Deep feeling of sharing the suffering of and the inclination to give support to another.

Dalai Lama Reincarnated spiritual and political leader of Tibet.

Druids Ancient order of priests in Britain.

Eckankar Religion of the Light and Sound of God.

Glossary

enlightenment. To give knowledge or truth; to endow with spiritual understanding.

guru An influential or revered teacher.

gnosis (Greek) Knowledge and wisdom.

hatha yoga Branch of yoga in which the practitioner does postures called asanas for increased health and well-being.

Hinduism Major religion of India.

Homer Greek epic poet and author of *The Iliad* and *The Odyssey.*

incense Scented stick that is sometimes burned during meditation to create a pleasant aroma.

Islam Major religion based on the teachings of Mohammed.

Judaism Religion based on ethical principles laid down in the Old Testament of the Bible and the Talamud.

Kabbalah Mystical teachings based on Jewish scriptures.

Lakota American Indian nation now located in South Dakota.

lama (Tibetan) Spiritual master.

mantra Repetition of sounds or words to aid in meditation.

medicine In Native American culture, medicine refers to the spiritual power of an object, plant, or animal.

Meditation

medicine man/medicine woman Native American healer and spiritual leader.
meditation Quieting the mind to attain higher states of consciousness.
meridian Lines along which energy flows in the body as described in the practice of Eastern and Chinese medicine.
mindfulness Bringing a high level of awareness to ordinary experience while remaining neutral.
object of meditation Focus of a meditation.
om Mystical utterance that contains all sounds within it.
pagani Ancient word meaning country dweller.
Plato Greek philosopher who lived around 400 BC.
Q'ero South American Indian tribe of the Andean Highlands.
quies Rest and peace; a state of heightened awareness sought of early Christian monks.
Rinpoche Same as lama.
Sanskrit Classical language of India.
shaman Human mediator between the spiritual and material worlds.
Siddhartha Buddha's birth name.
tai chi Chinese system of exercises for self-defense and meditation that is concerned with chi, an invisible energy that flows in the body.

Glossary

Tunkashila (Lakota) Great Spirit or God.

visualization Formation of mental images.

vodoun Religion of African origin practiced mainly in Haiti and characterized by rituals in which participants communicate with saints, ancestors, and animistic deities; also known as voodoo.

Wicca Contemporary religion based on practices of ancient nature worship and invocation of the Great Goddess.

yoga Term that means union with the divine. A general term for the Indian practice of meditations, diet, postures, and lifestyle leading to higher states of consciousness.

Zen Branch of Buddhism practiced in Japan.

For More Information

In the United States

Insight Meditation Society
1230 Pleasant Street
Barre, MA 01005
(978) 355-4378
Web site: http://www.dharma.org/ims.htm

Mind/Body Medical Institute
Beth Israel Deaconess Medical Center
Harvard Medical School
110 Francis Street
Boston, MA 02215
(617) 632-9530
Web site: http://www.mbmi.org

For More Information

In Canada

Canadian Tibetan Buddhist Society
758 Scotland Avenue
Winnipeg, MB R3M 1X6
(204) 775-8123
e-mail: disaac@icenter.net
Web site: http://www.mts.net/~ctbs

Web Sites

http://www.dharma.org
This site has information on insight meditation.

http://www.dzogchen.org
This site has information on Dzogchen meditation.

http://www.eckankar.org
This site has information on Eckankar.

http://www.sivananda.org/meditati.htm
This site has information on yoga.

For Further Reading

Benson, Herbert. *The Relaxation Response.* Richmond, VA: Outlet Books, Inc., 1993.

Davich, Victor N. *The Best Guide to Meditation.* Los Angeles: Renaissance Books, 1998.

McGaa, Ed Eagle Man. *Mother Earth Spirituality: Native American Paths to Healing Ourselves and Our World.* San Francisco, CA: Harper & Row, 1990.

Roche, Lorin. *Meditation Made Easy.* San Francisco, CA: Harper Collins, 1998.

Thoreau, Henry David. *Walking.* Berkeley, CA: The Nature Company, 1993.

Index

A
acupuncture, 19
affirmations, 35–39
Allogenes, 31
asanas, 26

B
Buddha, 8, 9, 26–27
Buddhism/Buddhists, 8, 18, 26, 27–28, 32, 52

C
Campbell, Joseph, 25
chakras, 19–20, 23
chanting, 10, 17, 30, 33, 48
Christianity, 28, 30, 32–33
creative visualization, 10, 21–22, 28, 29, 30, 48

D
Druids, 32

E
Eckankar, 18, 29

G
Gnosticism, 32

H
hatha yoga, 26
Hinduism, 18, 26

I
Ishtar, worshippers of, 32
Islamic meditation, 32

J
Judaism, 32
Jung, Carl, 29

K
Kabbalah, 32

L
lotus position, 15

M
manifestation, 22
mantras, 17, 30, 33

meditation
  developing a daily practice, 13–15
  explanation of, 7–8, 9–12, 16
  goals of, 7, 10, 39
  origins/history of, 25–34
meditation exercises
  affirmation meditation, 38
  breathing to reduce stress, 44–45
  chanting hu, 18–19
  creative visualization for freedom from fear, 42–44
  creative visualization/an inner guide for wisdom, 53–55
  creative visualization for reaching a goal, 22–24
  creative visualization for success in athletics, 40–41
  creative visualization in the garden of happiness, 49–51
  dealing with difficult people, 46–47
  mantra chanting, 18
  meditation in action, 52
  stilling the mind, 12–13
  walking meditation, 51–52
meridians, 19, 26
mindfulness, 9, 48, 52

N
New Age meditation, 29
North and South American Indians, meditation techniques used by, 33–34

T
third eye, 19, 20
transcendental meditation, 29

W
Wicca, 30–31

Y
yoga, 10, 15, 19, 26
Yogi, Maharishi, 29

About the Author

Judith Sainte Croix is an author, musician, and classical composer of new music. She enjoys meditating and has a Web site at http://www.judithsaintecroix.com/meditation. She lives in New York City.

Photo Credits

Cover, p. 21 © Index Stock; pp. 11, 27, 49 © FPG; p. 7 © Associated Press; pp. 14, 36, 45 © Corbis; p. 31 © Adriana Skura; Diagram on p. 20 by Nelson Sa.

Designer

Nelson Sá

www.ingramcontent.com/pod-product-compliance
Lightning Source LLC
Chambersburg PA
CBHW041114070526
44584CB00002B/166